A Choice Tl

Happiness

How To Make Yourself Happy

Carleen Glasser

From the "Choice Theory in Action Series"

ISBN: 9781071219164

First Published by Amazon, June 2019

Dedicated to

My husband
William Glasser
in loving memory
of the happiness we shared

CONTENTS

The Choice Theory In Action Series

This is one of a series of short books aimed at helping people gain better control of their lives using ideas from Choice Theory psychology, a theory of human behaviour that was developed by Reality Therapy creator Dr. William Glasser.

In this selection of books we explain the application of Choice Theory psychology to a range of popular themes such as   Addiction, Anger, Depression, Happiness, Parenting, Relationships, and Stress. The authors are all experts in Choice Theory psychology and all have studied directly under its creator, Dr. William Glasser.

Carleen Glasser, the author of this book about Happiness, has always been in a privileged position to understand Choice Theory. She had taught it for many years but she was also married to Dr. Glasser.   This psychology was not simply some academic theory but something they lived in their everyday lives together.   They shared the teaching, the teasing out of new aspects of the theory and, most important of all, living a life and relationship based on Choice Theory.

Hopefully this book will help you see happiness in a new way, one that helps you iive a fuller life and share that happiness with those around you.

Brian Lennon
Series Editor

Acknowledgments

The first person I want to thank is William Glasser, my late, dear husband and partner of twenty wonderful years. For sharing with me his unconditional love and his vast knowledge of humankind, I will be grateful the rest of my life. Bill's ideas were and still are a source of inspiration and growth for me. I will always remember the beautiful relationship we chose to have together. With this little book I am attempting to share his belief that, happiness is a choice.

I am extremely pleased to have been asked to write this book as a part of a series conceived and organized by, Brian Lennon. His work teaching and promoting the Glasser ideas has spread throughout Ireland and connected people from all over the world. Bill Glasser often said of Brian, "He's a good man and I am very lucky to have him on my team." Dr. Glasser had so much faith in Brian that he invited him to organize and Chair the first International William Glasser Institute.

I would also like to acknowledge Dr. Robert E. Wubbolding, my great mentor, who first introduced me to Reality Therapy in his Counseling Class at Xavier University, Cincinnati, Ohio in 1983. Dr. Wubbolding has created a system for teaching and delivering Reality Therapy called W.D.E.P. and has written numerous books and articles explaining Glasser's work. Bob and his wife Sandie Wubbolding, introduced me to Bill Glasser and I thank them both for what became for me the adventure of a lifetime.

My heartfelt thanks goes to the creative folks who agreed to share their personal stories about the happiness they have experienced in their lives for publication in this book. Through what they shared, I was able to explain Dr. Glasser's Choice Theory and offer ways for people who read this book to implement these ideas in their lives.

The contributors are, in alphabetical order:

Antionette Asimus
Mary Beth Barry
Shearon Bogdanovic
Susan Floyd Doolittle
Billie Fischer
Deirdre Gainor
Jullian Goldstein
Ellery Hollsapple
Maki Izumi
Rose-Inza Kim
Maria Lee
Brian Lennon
Terrence McWilliams
Roger Samuel
Judy Sinjur
Everne Spiegel
Mark Thompson
Lester Triché
RoxAnne Triché
Steve Wallace

Preface: Happiness, A New Perspective

How would you define happiness? When and how have you experienced happiness in your lifetime?

Defining happiness is difficult. Finding two snowflakes that look alike would be easier. At best you can observe happiness in yourself and possibly in others as a pleasurable feeling, a positive state of mind or a chosen behavior. An example of happiness, as a chosen behavior, is the familiar phrase "laughing on the outside, crying on the inside."

William Glasser worked with delinquent girls, early in his career, as Psychiatrist at the Ventura School for Girls in California. He often asked the girls who were complaining about being detained there and wanted to get out, "What would you need to be doing for them to let you out?" They almost all answered, " I'd have to be good. " To this he would reply, "Well then, could you, just for now, pretend to be good?"

The girls who did this, changed with the choice to act good. They ultimately became what they were pretending to be. They discovered that in choosing a more effective behavior, they got more of what they wanted and were happier than they seemed to be before.

Needless to say, I am not going to define happiness in this booklet because it is different for each person. We may have all heard the saying, "One man's trash is another man's treasure." Happiness is what we individually perceive it to be for ourselves.

In this booklet I have collected perceptions of personal happiness written by people of all ages and from their various and unique perspectives. I will then explain how Dr. Glasser's Choice Theory ideas were illustrated by the author of each story and I will suggest ways you can apply these ideas in your own life. I call these suggestions A Choice Theory Take Away.

Here is a brief summary of the Choice Theory Ideas you will hear about as I explain how they were demonstrated in each story. First, Choice Theory explains Our Universal Basic Needs. Everyone is born with needs that are part of their genetic instructions. The five basic needs each of us arrive with are:

1. SURVIVAL
2. LOVE and BELONGING
3. POWER
4. FREEDOM
5. FUN

We all have these same needs but they vary in strength from individual to individual. For example, you may have a high need for love and belonging and a low need for freedom. If your spouse has a low need for love and belonging and a high need for freedom, the two of you may have problems in your marriage because your need strengths are incompatible. As Dr. Glasser's wife, I co-authored a book with him about compatibility in relationships called, *Getting Together and Staying Together, Solving the Mysteries Marriage.*

Observe in your family how infants and children behave when they are not getting their basic needs met. They can be quite persistent in trying to convince someone to give them what they need. They are internally motivated by their needs and need strengths to attempt to control you and everything their environment has to offer in order to get what they want. You will hear more about this later.

The second explanation of human behavior in Choice Theory is what Dr. Glasser decided to call: THE QUALITY WORLD.   You may be asking, "What's that? And where is it?"

The human brain has the uncanny ability to recognize and store information. Our memories are like a savings account at the bank where deposits and withdrawals are made at our discretion. Your Quality World is a small part of the place were your memories are kept. We keep pictures in our Quality World of ourselves and other important people, places, things and systems of belief like politics or religion. These pictures are our version of what will satisfy our basic needs. Dr. Glasser made a point of stressing that the Quality World is not anyone else's version of what should or should not be there to fit some standard the external world has set up. We, alone, have full control over what we put in our Quality World and what we take out.

Throughout our lives we are driven by these pictures to get what we want and we are constantly comparing our unique pictures with what the real world is offering us. When the real world pictures do not match the pictures in our Quality World, we are frustrated and experience an urgent, internal motivation to force a match. We feel a compulsion to behave to change reality, as we see it, to match our internal pictures of what we want. The only other option is to adjust our pictures somewhat or take them out of our Quality World all together and replace them with more realistic or more attainable pictures.

The third explanation of Dr.Glasser's Choice Theory involves choosing our behaviors to deal with our frustrations. Dr.Glasser says, "all behavior is chosen and it is our best attempt at the time to get our needs met." He describes what we do as using Total Behavior. That is, Feeling, Physiology, Thinking and Acting all occurring simultaneously to accurately describe our behavior. Think of Total Behavior as four wheels of a car. The back wheels are all about feelings, both physical and emotional. The front wheels are about our thoughts and our actions, which take the car in some direction towards getting what we want. If our front wheels succeed our back wheels follow right along and we feel better. Choosing to take charge of our front wheels, Acting and Thinking which we can control, has a better chance of achieving happiness than staying stuck in painful emotional or physical feelings over which we have no direct control.

Creativity is the fourth dimension of Choice Theory. If we have a problem and have to figure out a solution, our Creative System is always there, day and night, to offer us new choices of behavior. That's the beauty of choice, because built into the word is the opportunity to make other or more effective choices. Creativity is tricky though. It can offer very effective solutions or it could offer very crazy or bizarre ideas. We can be creative in all four components of our behavioral system, as in creative feelings, creative physiology, creative thoughts and creative actions. The up-side is, we always have the choice to accept or reject these creative behaviors.

Creativity is also genetic. Some people are just born with a talent through which they express their creativity. For example, in chapter 3, Terrence, was born with the talent to become a musician. Perhaps somewhere in his gene pool were musicians or maybe he simply loved the musical sounds he heard as an infant and placed music in his Quality World. Nature or nurture? Creativity can appear in many forms in all of us. We are all creative and have talents that can be discovered at any age, if we look for them in our Quality Worlds.

In this booklet I will explain Choice Theory in the context of the stories I have collected. It is my hope that you, the readers, will see yourselves in these stories and begin to understand Choice Theory through them.   The purpose of this booklet is to give you some new tools to find what choices you could make to be happier than you are now.

1. Am I Happy?

Deirdre Gainor

I woke thinking about your question, what is happiness to me? I saw through the slats in the shade that the sun had begun to paint the sky a new day but it was not yet time to rise. I pulled the light blanket over my shoulder and rolled onto my side. Is this happiness?

I sat on my couch at the end of the work day, no lists, no worries, no yearning, just me on the couch feeling the warmth of the lowering sun on my neck. I looked around the room, familiar, present but also still. In this moment there are no demands. My lungs expand and I bow to being alive. Is this happiness?

It was still dark when we got to the beach. We could hear the swish of the oars in the channel as the crew chanted their strokes, one solitary light on their bow showing the way. As we walked out onto the sand, wet from the tide, the seals on the rocks began to call to each other in short sharp barks. We walked quietly along the water's edge until the uphill knee began to complain then turned and headed back. The sky was beginning to lighten over the channel and we could see the tops of the masts making their way to the sea. Is this happiness, I thought?

He walks in the door, six feet five inches, tall, handsome, smiling and bends to give me a hug. Our son, home from a trip abroad, comes to sit in the back yard, eat ratatouille, made fresh with tomatoes from the garden, and share his adventures. Happiness?

I sit at the table, a cup of tea beside me, with my writing book open. The dog sleeps in the bed at my feet. Pen poised. Write what you will, I say. Happiness?

I reach into my purse, the new one you gave me for my birthday. You shouldn't have. It was too good for me. I hid it in my closet for six weeks now, wondering when the time, the moment, the occasion would warrant such a purse and my fingers touched something disgusting, slimy, and rotten. You had put in a peach, the perfect reminder of our time last summer but I hadn't opened it, unwilling to allow myself to own such a beautiful thing and now I had ruined it, the silk lining moldy and stained. I burst into tears. Sad and happy, for all the love in my life. I just have to figure out how to take it in.

Choice Theory Reflections

Deirdre's happiness is expressed in the poetry of a creative mind. She beautifully describes how everyday life can be contemplated and perceived as happiness. In Deirdre's perception, her life is happy for all the love in it. Sadness may creep in occasionally in any life, but happiness is a choice we make even when we experience some sadness.

Choice Theory states that everyone perceives the world differently. There are three levels of perception, positive (pleasurable), negative (painful) and neutral (neither of the above). A lot of our happiness depends upon our choice of how we perceive the world around us at any given time.

A Choice Theory Take Away

There is an old saying, "When life hands you lemons, (you can choose to) make lemonade!" Learning to reframe the negative into a positive is one of life's most helpful skills when you are choosing to be happy. Practice using this skill by observing the next thing that happens to you that you feel unhappy about. Then try to see one part of it as a plus now or at least useful later. What did you learn from the experience that you can use another time?

Sometimes, as in Deirdre's peach in the purse example trying to find a thought to reframe it to the positive is very difficult. She burst into tears then added, "Sad and happy, for all the love in my life." That kind of sums up the whole Choice Theory concept of reframing a perception to the positive . Focus on the good relationships you have in your life. They will get you through any lemons you have been handed or rotten peaches you find.

2. Just Direct Your Feet to the Sunny Side of the Street

Judy Sinjur

HAPPINESS DEFINITION, WEBSTER: Noun, the state of being happy. Synonyms: pleasure, contentment, satisfaction, cheerfulness, merriment, gaiety, joyfulness, jollity, glee, delight, good spirits, lightheartedness, well – being, enjoyment and more.

Just so you know where I am starting from, I already know that I get to choose to be happy(the glass is full) or sad (the glass is empty). Also, I know that I almost always choose to feel happy.This still doesn't define or explain what happiness is and how or why someone would what to be happy.

When I make a mistake of some sort that gets me all worked up, angry or sad, like, I say something to someone that I can't take back for whatever reason, how do I forgive myself and move forward? If another person, say a child is involved, how do you begin to be at peace with what just happened vs. beating yourself up or getting depressed? I start by finding at least one thing, animal, color, person etc. that will put a smile on my face or amaze me or make me laugh. When I go back to where I came from (the state I was in when I got angry at myself or made the mistake) I am able to look for the answer or possible resolution with new fresh eyes and heart. Many times just the fact that I was able to calm myself down enough to use my own wherewith all, that makes me happy (gives me joy, or some type of satisfaction, happiness.

Sometimes when I go walking for exercise, I say, " Hello" to perfect strangers I meet along the way to see how many I can find who say hi back to me or smile;   that increases my happiness knowing that for all intent and purposes something I did gave them a little happiness or put a smile on their face in that moment.

Seeing humming birds we feed fly all around the feeder playing, makes me happy and relaxes me. I think of them when I get to work. I arrive with a smile, which could possibly make someone else who has had a rough morning smile or get on a path to feeling happier. This makes me happy and keeps me happy for the rest of the day. If I choose to get angry with my spouse in the morning and I choose to talk to him about why I got angry, I am happy with myself for keeping our evening together pleasant vs. stressed and tense from the morning's conversation.

Happiness comes from within. How do you want to present yourself to the world each day? Happiness may be presenting yourself   in a positive manner and helping someone else to find happiness in their day. Sometimes happiness is just waking up in the morning. Sometimes happiness is very difficult to find.   It is at that time that I fall back on remembering the phrase, "I HAVE A CHOICE". The choice to find happiness on many given days may be difficult but if you succeed, just for a moment, you can maybe capture it for two moments the next day and more the day after that.

Even if it's only a piece of glass that captured the sun sending a stream of light that filled your heart with wonder, hold it in your mind to think of whenever you are down. This is what I do for myself and it's even better if I am with someone else. Together we find a flower blooming, a cloud in the sky that has the shape of an animal, a sunset that is stunning, a line of ants scurrying to do whatever they do. I solve a riddle, answer a math problem correctly find my car in the parking garage and on and on storing a stock pile of happy thoughts that trigger happy feelings. These are beautiful memories that sustain me.

Choice Theory Reflections

Judy is using the concept in Choice Theory of creating positive perceptions by what she chooses to let into her mind through her five senses. Whatever she senses, she identifies as something she knows and something she likes because it matches one of her ideal pictures in her Quality World. She practices retaining these positive perceptions and finding more to add to them in order to keep her emotional world in balance.

She is constantly creating a stockpile of pleasurable perceptions to sustain her through the times when her happiness is challenged. She uses them to give her the strength to make choices that help her instead of choices that could ultimately hurt her and prevent her from being happy. Judy acknowledges, no one is happy all the time and her most unhappy times are when she gets angry at herself. But, note, when this anger swells in her, she, unlike many others, chooses to take a little detour into her happy-thoughts-place to buy herself some time to calm down and figure out a more effective way to handle her anger.

The beauty of Choice Theory is that everyone gets to define Happiness for themselves because it is a choice. But, what part does the world outside of us play in making us happy? All we can get from the outside world is information and all we can give to someone else besides ourselves is information. So, following this line of thought, the apparent flaw in the question is the word "MAKE". Can I make you happy without your permission? Have you ever desperately tried to make someone happy who was having none of it no matter what you did or said? It is very disappointing to most people to give up the word "MAKE" in this context, because it means giving up control which is part of fulfilling our need for Power.

External control is rooted in our need for Power. Believing you can make someone happy or sad or angry and conversely they can control you by making you depress or filled with joy seems logical but fails the test of consistency. Maybe you have experienced it on occasion and it felt plausible that something outside yourself "made" you happy. The fact is we all choose how we perceive the world and compare those perceptions from the Real World with our Quality World pictures. If there is a match we are satisfied . If there is not a match we are unhappy. Happy people put pictures in their Quality Worlds that they believe will have a good chance of matching what they perceive in the Real World. Happy people evaluate their pictures of what they want and their choices of behavior to achieve what they want.

A Choice Theory Take Away

The next time you are frustrated or upset, try this Choice Theory idea that Judy uses. You can change your perceptions from being negative or panful by re-thinking the information the real world is offering you. Whatever anyone says to you and whatever you say to them is just information. For example, if you become angry because someone insults you, what you would say to yourself is, this information is false and no one can control me with their insults by making me mad. I choose my own thoughts.

Since all behavior is a choice, you can choose to neutralize your perceptions of someone or something by replacing these thoughts with other more pleasant thoughts of your own that you have stored in your memory. Then you are in control. You evaluate your own behavior. No one can control you without your permission. Refuse to give away your power by believing someone made you mad. Change that perception and you will be free to live a happy life. And always remember, unhappy people spend an inordinate amount of time evaluating other people. Happy people only evaluate themselves.

3. Happiness is Music to My Ears

Terrence McWilliams

Happiness to me… is being a professional musician. My love of music started early, at the age of four years old, listening to music from films. Then fourteen years later I enrolled in Berklee College of Music in Boston, Massachusetts, where my major was Composition and Film Scoring. My favorite class was listening and analysis, confirming the old saying, "The apple doesn't fall far from the tree".

My first exposure to instruments was when I was about seven years old. My maternal Grandmother Heimbach, whom I called "Mutie" gave me a ukulele and "Dah", my Grandfather Heimbach gave me a harmonica. From there I couldn't wait to move up to guitar and various wind instruments. My wonderful Grandparents, whom I loved so much, had started something that would spark my interest for the rest of my life.

As an elementary classroom teacher, I was teaching a class in Music Appreciation, but I decided to change the name to Music Awareness. Music can be anything hit, strummed, plucked blown or sung. Music is all around us, birds chirping, wind through the leaves, ocean waves on the beach, traffic noise. Just listen and enjoy.

Composer, John Cage walked onto the stage, sat down at the piano and the piece of music he offered was the random sounds of moving chairs, rustling papers, coughing and a murmuring audience. I play music on my instruments, guitar, bass, clarinet, wood flutes and piano to entertain audiences but mostly for my own satisfaction and enjoyment.

As well as performing classic rock, southern rock and Celtic rock, professionally, I enjoyed playing with a Boston based band, The Found Percussion Orchestra. The instruments consisted of hub caps, trash bin lids, wood and pieces of metal. It had multimedia visuals, strobe lights, dance and shadows. I played guitar and did sound effects for the performances.

Dr. William Glasser heard me perform my arrangement of heavy metal traditional Celtic music and commented that he could hear the passion in my music and that this was a labor of love. It is living what I love. He and his comments meant a great deal to me.

I heard about a 99 year old woman, who played in a symphony orchestra. She passed away during a rehearsal, literally doing what she loved until the day she died. And Then there is Beethoven, who wrote his 9th symphony when completely deaf. The music was in his head! He could not hear the standing ovation at the end of the performance so the 1st violinist got up and turned him around to see the applauding audience.

All in all, music is in my head and it makes me happy. It gives me a sense of accomplishment, fulfillment, gratification and purpose in life. It also means to me, communication with other musicians and a connection with the audiences for whom I perform. Music is academically stimulating with the study of acoustics of music, physics, numbers and patterns. Through creative expression, with music, I am very happy with what I do.

Choice Theory Reflections

One's Quality World contains pictures of people, things and systems of belief that are perceived to be need satisfying now or potentially need satisfying in the future. They motivate all of our behavior. Music, for Terrence, is in the thing category, but is also very much a part of his creative system and his life.

In Terrence's Quality World, he has a very large and prominent picture of all things related to music. He was born with a talent for music and his entire life from childhood on has been filled with music. I witnessed this phenomenon because I am his Mother.

My son, Terrence is one of those unique individuals who hears music within and can reproduce what he hears in his head through a musical instrument. He plays most string instruments like guitar, both electric and acoustic, bass guitar, banjo and dulcimer. He also plays the wind instruments such as various wood flutes, clarinet and saxophone. He has recently taught himself to play piano. Terrence has composed, arranged and scored music for films. He teaches music and sees music as a large part of his purpose in life.

Because of the genetic instructions to fulfill our basic needs for love and belonging, power, or freedom and fun, music is Terrence's vehicle for getting all his needs met. If he needs more love and belonging he plays music for and with people. Performance and recognition of his talent for music fulfills his need for power. His freedom need is met by the mere act of choosing what to play and how he wants to play it. Music for Terrence is continually satisfying and a new learning experience which meets his need for fun. He has earned money for performing and teaching thus contributing to his survival need but more than that, Terrence could not thrive without his music. Terrence has had himself, as a musician, in his Quality World his entire life and fulfilling that picture is his happiness.

A Choice Theory Take Away

Take a look at the pictures you put in your Quality World. Do they include a picture you placed there, doing something, that fulfills every one of your Basic Needs? In all likelihood, that picture will motivate every component of your behavior, because it is need satisfying in every way.

If you have a particular talent or strong passion for anything, your Creative System is usually involved. Dr. Glasser advised us to "Trust your Creative System." What he meant by that is, your Creative

System never stops working. It even works while you are asleep. Have you ever awakened in the morning with the solution to yesterday's problem that had suddenly popped into your head the minute you opened your eyes? That's your creativity working.

If your Creative System offers you an idea to do something like act, think, and feel something new, listen to it, but first ask yourself a very important question. Ask if what you would choose to do will help or hurt your chances of you getting your needs met.

If the answer is a resounding yes, then you may have found, like Terrence, your talent or driving force in life.

4. In All Kinds of Weather We Stick Together

Antoinette Asimus

Happiness to me is a feeling of inner warmth, contentment and a sense that all is well both inside myself and, at least in that moment, in the outside world.   Picture, taste and feel smooth honey melting on the tongue, as, with its B vitamins, it nourishes and calms soul and body.   Picture, feel and smell a rainstorm blowing in to shift unbearably hot and muggy days to cool, clear, dry air as it brings relief to soul and body.

Reading and books open opportunities for me to experience happiness.   My first memories of experiencing this happiness was as a toddler, either nestled on my mother's lap, or snuggled closely at her side as she read a book of nursery rhymes to me.   Even after learning to read for myself, I begged my mother to read to me.   I loved the closeness and warmth of her body, the rhythms in her voice as she read and the pictures in my mind as the stories unfolded.

In the last year of her life my mother told me that when I was a toddler, I did not have a security blanket as many other children did.   Instead, I had the book of nursery rhymes that she read to me. She said I carried it with me everywhere I went until page by page fell away and the book disappeared. But then I entered first grade which was such an exciting year for me as I solved the puzzles of letters and sounds coming together to form words.

Another bonus from learning to read was discovering the public library. Not only did I love the smell of the library and the feel of the books, I loved being able to borrow stacks of books to take home and savor from cover to cover, like warm honey melting at the back of my mind as it nourished my soul.

It wasn't until I was in high school that I discovered one could buy books and create a library of one's own. The idea that I could create my own library, sparked a lifelong joy of reading book reviews, visiting bookstores, attending writers' readings of their work, joining book discussions and again in a variety of ways experiencing the happiness that reading and books bring me.

Have I ever felt less than happy with books? Yes. When I downsized my belongings to move from my 10 room home to a condominium, I felt perplexed sadness as I had to choose which of my best friends to sell or give away before I moved. Sixty boxes of books moved out of my house to new homes, while a remaining sixty boxes of books moved with me to my new condo. Like a rainstorm blowing in to shift unbearably hot and muggy days to cool, clear, dry air bringing relief to soul and body.

Choice Theory Reflections

I know this writer very well, for she, I am proud to say, is my sister. We grew up in the same house with the same parents but we are two entirely unique and different people. Genes we share in common are more alike than with any other human being on earth. We both have a high genetic predisposition to fulfill our love and belonging need. Antoinette has the highest need for love and belonging I have ever witnessed in our family. She is the one, of the two of us, who keeps track of all our cousins and knows everything on record about our ancestors.

Choice Theory explains internal motivation as being driven by our universal basic needs to get what we want. We all are born with them but individually we have various strengths of each need. The need strengths are what I was alluding to when I said Antoinette has a very high need for love and belonging. By that I mean she both needs to be loved but she also needs to love and belong. Since she is such a high achiever, she also has a high need for power and control, which manifests in her as accomplishments and achievements not control over others. Her joy in learning indicates a strong need for fun, the genetic reward for learning. Her survival and freedom needs show up in her tendency to be careful with her health and money and in her need to be an independent and creative thinker.

She is a living encyclopedia of anything I might need to know. All that time spent in libraries did not go to waste. She is a lifelong learner and because of that, Choice Theory explains, she has a high need for Fun. I can attest to that. When we are together we tend to laugh a lot and discuss everything from the problems of the world to our last shopping trip purchases. Food is also big on our list of topics to discuss.

Antoinette is Reality Therapy and Choice Theory Certified and she employs these skills, among others, as a professional trainer and certified coach helping people solve the mysteries of their relationships. She has been recognized as a leader in her field and is currently a political activist for causes that inspire and move her. She has many opportunities to fulfill her power need and she is very adept at doing so graciously and without using external control.

All those hours Antoinette spent cuddled with our mother reading books created a warm hearted, loving sister for me to cherish for the rest of my days. Luckily for both of us our Mother was an equal opportunity reader and I got my share of what my sister experienced. But the one thing our Mother felt strongest about was that the two of us stay closely connected and she would be pleased to know, we have.

A Choice Theory Take Away

Never underestimate the power of staying connected with your siblings. In the end they are the closest living creatures on this earth to you. We all come into the world alone and essentially leave it alone, but while we are here, no matter what has happened between you and your siblings in the past, you share the same life force within you and you are better together than you are alone. Whenever I am lonely or need to talk to someone or hear a familiar sounding voice I call my sister. Sometimes, I could be thinking about calling her and the phone rings.

She's calling me from 3000 miles away. How did she know? She followed her inner voice, which Choice Theory explains as the source of all of our choices. We are all internally motivated to behave, driven by pictures of what we want in our Quality World. If you have a place in anyone's Quality World you need not be in front of them in person for them to be thinking of you precisely at the time you are thinking of them. If you and your siblings make the effort to stay in each other's Quality Worlds, you may never feel   lonely again. You will have a greater chance of being happy because happy people rarely feel lonely for long. The phone will always ring. It is your choice to answer it.

5. Keys to Happiness

Susan Floyd Doolittle

I had the wonderful privilege of putting my eight year old son, Nicholas to bed on Christmas Eve. My daughter Scarlett, six, was carried off to bed by her daddy, already asleep. Or at least pretending to be.

I read three books that night, snuggled side by side with Nicholas in his soft twin bed. 'The Twelve Days Of Christmas', 'We Wish You A Merry Christmas', and 'The Polar Express'. After I read the last line of the last book, I closed the book softly, placed it on the floor, turned off the reading light, and snuggled with my child. I smiled to myself in the darkness as I felt Nicholas kiss my cheek. We lay in silence for many minutes listening to the stillness, the magic of Christmas Eve. I turned my head to Nicholas, I saw his beautiful face next to mine in the warm blue glow of his air purifier's dim light. We gazed at each other....then softly...."Merry Christmas Nicholas"...."Merry Christmas Mama". He shut his eyes. A sob filled my heart. I then felt electricity filling my veins with... happiness...... Can it be contained in a single word? Joy, awe, gratitude, contentment, peace, nature, spirituality ...rapture. My happiness is never alone. My happiness always welcomes other emotions over for company.

My mother, Carleen Glasser, asked me to contribute to this book. I put it off. I'm a busy mom! I am happy. I have a wonderful husband and two terrific kids. I am too busy to think of happiness most days...I just am, happy. I'm a nice, thoughtful, caring, generous person... I'm friendly. I assume people mostly think of me as happy. I have a lot of worries too. Real worries about myself and my loved ones, so even though I have a wonderful family, I am not sure I am actually feeling deeply happy as much as I could, should or wish. For me happiness comes out as epiphanies or bolts of lightning.

When I notice my happiness, or give it my FULL attention, it is usually accompanied with sadness. Tears of joy? My happiness understands that in order for me to let it in, it must allow all of my inner world to experience it too, and vice versa. When I am fully present, all aspects of my being at full attention, it's like being in the presence of something greater than myself. My sadness IS my happiness. The fact that I feel sad, mad, frightened, joyous, grateful...makes me understand that I care. The fact that I care makes me happy. I choose to allow these feelings to pass through me like a wave. I love them.

I am standing center stage, it is the last performance of St. Joan. I have given countless performances, for thousands of people, I am proud, I am overwhelmed, exhausted. I fully understand that I have used my body and mind for what they were made for.   I feel totally at one with myself, I am present, I have   talent, I am flying, my whole body feels it.   The feelings crush me, lift me, spin me. I take a bow, and another and another ..... happiness, sadness.

I am holding Brian's hand.   We are in my parents living room surrounded by family and friends. We are being married.   I am squeezing his hand, he is squeezing mine, we are gazing into each others eyes, speaking the words, bodies trembling, on the verge of letting go.... no hold your tears, I've got you.   We are excited, frightened, grateful. Happy.

I am walking on the treadmill in our home, I gaze at a picture of William Glasser on the wall. I am full of gratitude, joy, and love.   I remember him making "Susan Salads" for us at dinner.   I remember how much I loved this man who had not a materialistic bone in his body, yet became despondent when the 'Susan Salad' bowl broke and the total joy he expressed when I surprised him with another.   I felt respect, awe, happy, that I could be a glimpse of HIS happiness.   This gave me a jolt, a myriad of emotions washed over me as I deeply, overwhelmingly, understood that I was loved.   My memories of Bill always fill me with happiness and sadness. I miss him.

I felt happiness the day my mother adopted me. My mother holds one of the few keys to my total happiness. I chose to give it to her the day that we met when I was eleven.   I cannot reflect on the deep connection I have with my mother without a thousand emotions coming to join my happiness.

Four more keys belong to Brian, Nicholas, Scarlett and my dog, Josie. The days my children were born were the two absolute happiest, most incredulous days of my life. The sixth and the final key belongs to me. My key is the master key. Although sometimes it doesn't feel that way.

My happiness expresses itself as a symphony and each key unlocks a different composition. I choose to care. Caring connections make me happy, whether I'm connecting with nature, my inner self or others, and sometimes, my happiness flows through my eyes in tears. That's me.

Choice Theory Reflections

Susan has very large feelings. Her experience of happiness is a myriad of behaviors Choice Theory calls Total Behavior. Of the four components of Total Behavior, acting, thinking, feeling and physiology, Susan's complexity of feelings, both emotional and physical reign supreme. In observing her, one is never at a loss for knowing that she is feeling deeply. Since Glasser says, "All behavior is chosen" and since feelings, both physical and emotional, are behaviors, is Susan choosing her feelings? The answer is no, not directly. We choose the thinking and acting components of Total Behavior but until we become aware of what we are doing, it seems like our feelings just come over us.

In all the examples Susan gave when she experienced many feelings, both happy and sad, she was completely aware of why she was having these feelings. She was present in the moment and could identify what she was doing and why she felt the way she did. Many therapists will encourage you to be in touch with your feelings. Choice Theory goes beyond that and explains how knowing what you feel is useful in the process of deciding what you will choose to do about how you feel. If you feel unhappy and you know you are unhappy, this awareness alone is not helping you. If you can figure out what you want and how to achieve it, through your considered actions, you help yourself change unhappiness to happiness.

A Choice Theory Take Away

Your feelings are your friends. Don't be afraid of them. Talk to yourself about them or talk to someone you trust about them. Feelings are messengers in your brain, informing you if the pictures in your Quality Word are being matched in the real world.

Happiness can be felt holistically through your entire being. Feeling happy involves all your thoughts, your actions your emotions and your physiology. To increase your happiness awareness ask yourself the following questions everyday: Am I thinking happy thoughts today? Am I acting happy in the world today? Am I feeling happy inside today? Am I sensing my body as full of happiness today? If your answer to any of those questions is no, it tells you what area you will need to work on that day. Susan spoke of caring. Caring for your own well being as well as others is fertile ground for growing happiness.

6. Hallelujah and Amen

Lester Triché

It was years ago when I experienced my greatest level of unhappiness. I was attending a Sunday morning church service, listening to the pastor finish her sermon, when a soft, yet powerful voice spoke asking: "What did you learn from the message being preached?" It shocked me, this question entered my mind and I knew I heard it from God.

I was new to the Word of God, so new I could not find the book of Genesis or even the book of Revelations. I was hungry to learn the Word of God for myself. Unfortunately, my pastor was delivering a motivational, intense message that captured the attention of what appeared to be everyone in attendance.

There were hundreds of people present that day, I could hear them shouting: "Praise the Lord," "Hallelujah," "Teach the Word," and "Amen" throughout the entire sermon. I felt emotional, lost, concerned, and I felt I was missing something—deep down inside, I needed something but didn't know what it was or how to get it.

All I could remember from the message was, "Fake it until you make it."

Being a person who had recently rededicated my life to Christ, I could not connect to that message or determine how to relate it to my walk with Christ. I wanted more, not just a "motivational message." I remember thinking: "I am sick of preachers in my life and their various interpretations of the Bible." I continued to attend weekly services. Unfortunately for me, I was doing the same thing (complaining) and not doing anything to get what I wanted. Finally, I cried out to God, asking: "Will You teach me Your Word?

During this time, I was attending a conference in San Francisco, California. After checking into the hotel, I got to my room; sat on the side of the bed, still craving a desire to know God and His Word. At that moment, I opened a nightstand, and saw a green Bible.

I read that green Bible but, despite having earned several academic degrees, I felt challenged understanding it—perplexed by the number of "thees and thous," I was lost, feeling hopeless, I thought, I would never get to know God and His Word.

Finally, I opened a Yellow Pages telephone book. As I went through the book, I searched for Christian Book Stores, yearning for an "easy" to read Bible.

It seemed each clerk I spoke with asked the same question, "What kind of Bible do you want?" Heck, I didn't know. It was frustrating and depressing, wanting something and not knowing how to describe it. I said: "I am looking for a Bible—one like the preachers use. I want to learn how to study and learn about God for myself."

At last, one clerk suggested using the "NIV" (New International Version) Bible. I asked, "what is that?" He said, "It's a modern language Bible." I was excited and asked if they had a one. The answer was "No." What? Are you kidding me! I set my mind on getting that specific Bible.

I called one Bookstore after another. Finally, near Fisherman's Wharf, I found one. Now, all I needed was to get there, I set my plan. So, I called a cab, asked the driver to take me to that bookstore and wait—which he did (thank you, Jesus). I entered the store and was advised they only had one copy of that Bible and it was red. What? Red? Seriously? I really didn't want a red Bible but knew I needed it, so I purchased it; index tabs, paper, and a pen!

The driver took me back to my hotel room—I was so excited and was eager to read my new Bible, I thought I would never reach the hotel. When I entered the hotel room, I immediately read the Bible, placing tabs on what seemed like hundreds of pages, I was highlighting something in every section—it felt like all I read ministered to me in a way I never experienced.

Today, I teach Scripture Therapy and how to rightly divide and discern the Word of God, through our internet international TV show

www.scripturetherapycenter.com

to over 100 countries.

NOW, I can truly shout "Amen," and "Hallelujah!" about learning and teaching the Word of God.

Choice Theory Reflections

Whenever Dr. Glasser would give a lecture on Choice Theory, he would often be asked the question, "Where do my religious beliefs fit into your Choice Theory? In this story, Lester illustrates perfectly, what Choice Theory explains. Lester has scripture and Choice Theory in his Quality World where they co-exist compatibly in the way he teaches them.

The pictures we choose to place in our Quality World are from three categories, people, other things and systems of belief. Religious beliefs of every kind have been placed in the Quality Worlds of billions of people since the beginning of man's existence on earth.

These beliefs are and have been so powerful that they have driven whole societies of people to behave in every possible way to help the world and in certain instances to destroy it. Many wars have been fought over differing systems of belief and are still being fought today. But more people, the world over, find great solace and joy in connecting with beliefs they share in congregation with others.

Since religious beliefs satisfy so many needs, they can, if chosen, become a major part of the most inspirational and motivational force in the human brain, your Quality World. Look at Lester's journey to find spiritual satisfaction in his life. His every choice is influenced by and fulfilled by finding true meaning and faith for himself.

He is currently Choice Theory/Reality Therapy Certified and a Senior Instructor for the William Glasser Institute International. Training people to apply Choice Theory to their lives as part of his ministry, is so need-satisfying to him that it is a major source of his happiness in life.

A Choice Theory Take Away

In his work and theory, Dr. Glasser was very careful not to favor any one religion or system of belief over another. Choice Theory explains how the brain works and why people are internally motivated to behave. This behavior is always a personal choice based on what we perceive as information from the real world and what we want inside our Quality World. We are satisfied, or happy when these two match.

It is in keeping with Choice Theory to respect other's beliefs and never try to force our beliefs on anyone. Whatever our beliefs are, all we can give to anyone else is information. We can influence others with this information best, if we take the time to build a Choice Theory relationship with them. Les and his wife RoxAnne, who is also CT/RT certified, teach their scripture therapy program in exactly this way and together they create an environment for people to choose much happiness for themselves in this world. Their book, *Scripture Therapy and Choice Theory* (2018). Christian Faith Publishing. Meadville, PA. has been well received. It has the potential of helping people from all kinds of backgrounds and systems of belief.

7. Happy Together in Good Times and Bad

Maki Izumi

I met my husband sixteen years ago when as Japanese students, we were studying abroad for a short period, at UCLA. The very first moment I saw him, I knew that I had fallen in love with him. He is so sweet, funny, and faithful. Words cannot explain what a wonderful person he is. He is so kind to my family and friends too. We really love, trust and support each other, so we can talk about everything, like life, family, friends and work. I was inspired by his wonderful way of thinking and his points of view. It has been ten years since we got married.

Right after we got married, he quit his job because he was suffering from depression and took a rest to recover from it for a couple of months. I did not know about depression and the treatments that can help. We were totally lost and did not know what to do. He was sleeping like a log all day, so I sometimes checked whether he was still breathing or not.

He had been a director at an IT Company, in charge of sales, so he had to manage both members and sales. He worked from very early in the morning until late at night every day. At a meeting, his boss threw a laptop at him when his team sales did not perform and also said horrible things. His parents and I wanted him to quit his job but he did not listen to us because he was earnest and faithful to the company and his team. Also he did not want to give up, so he chose to keep working. One day, he had to give up his salary due to deteriorating performance then decided to quit his job. He made this decision by himself. I never thought that I wanted to break up with him.

The only thing that I could do was stay with him no matter what. I was worried about him but I knew how he felt and I did not want to blame him. He has always stood for me and supported me through the good times and the bad times, so I wanted to support him. We were just doing normal things like going for a walk with our dog, playing games at an amusement arcade, taking a nap, reading books in our favorite park and having a chat at a café. He was gradually getting better and could return to a normal life. He started to look for a new job that he really wanted to do and found a wonderful company. He has been working for that company for ten years and now he is so happy to contribute to the company, his team, customers and the society.

I understand that I am the only person who can protect myself both mentally and physically through his experience. Once we lose our balance, it is so difficult to recover and we have to spend a lot of money and time to get it back. The most important thing is that he taught me to be healthy mentally and be sure to take care of myself. Also we should notice any small signal when we feel something wrong with our body and mind. When he is pleased with his work, I feel happy even though he is very busy. We have gotten over it and now we are so happy together.

People that I love have taught me the importance of life, being healthy both mentally and physically. Also I have found what happiness is for me. I used to see things that I don't have and compare with others and I was depressed. I stopped comparing myself to others. I am really happy that I met my husband, with whom I want to spend the rest of my life. We would both love to have a child, but so far it has not happened. We are doing what we can, following medical advise and hope it will work, but I really appreciate that I just want to be with him. He is a gift of God.

Now I can see things that I have and I appreciate just being alive. I am grateful to wake up every morning with the thought that I am still alive today. Every year, I go to see my paternal grandmother who lives far away from our house. Last time when I met her, I asked "What's happiness for you?" Her answer was "I'm happy just to see you". I am so blessed to have such amazing people in my life. I can't wait to see what wonderful things await me in the future!

Choice Theory Reflections

In Choice Theory terms, Maki's story speaks for itself. Maki is choosing to live her life completely in the present. She is grateful for her beautiful relationships and even in the face of loss and disappointments she never gives up on anyone including herself.

In Chapter eleven, Julian speaks of "Natural Knowing". Maki seems to have been born with that gift of knowing how important staying close and connected is to experience happiness. No matter how difficult your burdens seem, having supportive relationships in your life will protect you from irreparable harm.

Maki has the natural knowing that using external control for example, the seven deadly habits will destroy any relationship she has and would like to keep. She is never seen Criticizing, Blaming, Complaining, Nagging, Punishing, Threatening or Rewarding to Control. Can you imagine what would have happened in her marriage if she had used any of those habits with her husband when he had his difficulties? What if Maki and her husband had blamed each other for their difficulty conceiving a baby? They would have both lost something very important in their lives, love for one another and possibly the beautiful relationship they share.

Dr. Glasser taught that there is only one problem in the world of mental health. The people who seek help are all unhappy. Why are they unhappy? They are unhappy because they lack need satisfying relationships in their lives, especially with themselves. Maki is a happy young woman and because she chooses to be happy, she brings joy to everyone she knows and meets.

A Choice Theory Take Away

Take a look at all the pictures in your Quality World. Dr. Glasser advises us to take any pictures of what we want out of our Quality World if they are unrealistic or could be harmful if we pursue them. An unrealistic picture could be as ridiculous as expecting to win the lottery when you never buy a ticket. A harmful picture could be expecting to lose 10 pounds to fit into a dress you want to wear on a date this weekend. Another unrealistic and harmful picture is expecting to be the life of the party by drinking alcohol until you are drunk and then driving your car home from the party. Evaluating your Quality World pictures, sorting them out as realistic or unrealistic, or potentially harmful and replacing these pictures with more realistic and helpful pictures could save your life and may even bring you more happiness if you pursue them.

8. To Dream the Impossible Dream

Mary Beth Barry

In 2012 I received the devastating news that I had end stage renal failure! I was living my life with my wonderful husband I married in 1973. I had two sons who I shared a lot of love with! My job was fun , meaningful, and rewarding! Friends Galore! I was dancing through life at every chance I had!

Renal failure came out of no where, no warning, no signs!

I needed to start dialysis right away! I made the decision to do the dialysis at home! It was a hard decision but the only one where I could do the process every night at home, and go to work every day. My husband , children and sister all tried to donate but no one was a match!

I made the decision not to tell anyone! Only my closest circle of family knew! I made the choice to live my life to the fullest exactly as I was and not waste a minute. I came to understand that I was not going to be able to find a kidney match because of my situation. I made the decision to prepare every day just in case I might get a kidney but not really believing it!

I was happy that Dialysis was available to help me! I sure focused on my wonderful doctor and the care he gave me! My miracle!

One morning when I never expected it I got a call from UCLA that they had a kidney!
I rushed to UCLA only to find out that it was true! A few hours later I had a functioning kidney!

Then in a state of pure joy I realized someone had died! I learned I had received a kidney from a young 29 year old professional athlete! He was a 95% match to me! Now he was 6ft tall and 260 pounds and I am 5 feet tall and 100 pounds!
How can you measure happiness when you receive a miracle? Why was I the one to receive this kidney! The stars were aligned and I was chosen to carry his kidney.

Choice Theory Reflections

Sometimes happiness comes in big packages! Mary Beth's story is about the need for survival, true, but, it is also about so much more. Surviving is one thing, choosing to live life to its fullest is the support system of happiness.

Mary Beth's story is an inspiration for maintaining hope in the face of a seemingly hopeless situation. Choosing to stay active and alive by thinking positive thoughts and finding effective actions to take keeps the momentum of life going. Choosing behaviors that you know will help you instead of ones that have a good chance of being ineffective or hurting you more is what practicing Choice Theory is all about.

Mary Beth did what she was able to do, directing the only things she had control over, her own thoughts and actions. She did not waste her time or energy trying to control what she had no control over. Some call it patience, that calm feeling you have when you give up trying to do the impossible and keep doing more of what is possible. Serenity is another name for what one feels when one chooses acceptance of the moment and staying in the present. Then, when you least expect it, a miracle like Mary Beth experienced might happen. Sometimes happiness is the miracle. Sometimes it comes as an unexpected surprise, especially when you just get out of the way and let it happen.

A Choice Theory Take Away

The next time you are challenged by a big problem, remember the four wheels on your behavioral car. If you are very upset about the problem you are usually focused on the back wheels of the behavioral car, Feelings and Physiology. You may feel anxious or angry or you may feel physical symptoms such as rapid heart beat or nausea. That is very understandable but you have very little or no control over any of these symptoms. The only way you can solve the problem or deal with it effectively, is to focus on your front wheels, Acting and Thinking. Thinking of something you can do, an action you can take or a plan you can make and commit to, are all behaviors that are under your control. Once you have come up with an effective way of dealing with the problem you will also have indirectly controlled the back wheel behaviors and their painful symptoms. Doing nothing is a choice. But, Choice Theory teaches that if you keep on doing what you've been doing you will keep on getting what you've got. You are in charge of your Total Behavior, both directly and indirectly. Happiness and misery are both choices within your control.

9. Everything I Thought I Knew

Ellery Holesapple

I was asked to write, briefly, how Choice Theory has impacted my life. I struggled with the word "briefly". Choice Theory has allowed me to shift my worldview. This process only required me to give up one thing – everything I thought I knew, especially about happiness. Choice theory encourages seven caring habits – this shift is simple, not easy. If I were to be successful in applying Choice Theory to myself I would need to unlearn the deadly habits I had adhered to all of my life. I was no longer going to be allowed to be critical, not only of others but of myself as well. I would no longer be able to blame this person or that person, the weather, or some other arbitrary thing for my behavior, my happiness, and or my sadness. I would no longer be a member of the complaining club – I hate Monday's etcetera.

Choice Theory freed me from the burden of nagging my friends, family, and children to do things. Additionally, I was no longer allowed to threaten, punish, or reward to control others. There would be no more quid pro quo. I would need to give these things up in order to experience the one-degree change that would lead me to a greater happiness. A simple task however; not an easy one as this paradigm was deeply entrenched in my upbringing as well as my culture.

To begin the paradigm shift towards happiness I would start by supporting and encouraging my friends, families, coworkers, colleagues, and random people on the street in whatever endeavor they were doing to meet their needs. This would require me to begin listening to what they wanted, not just "hear" what they were saying. Additionally, I would have to accept, trust, and respect their choices and how they went about meeting their needs. This does not mean I would have to agree with everything. Instead Choice Theory would give me the tools of negotiating differences to shed light on a different point of view.

Since my introduction to Choice Theory I have accepted my responsibility in making my world the way I want it to be. This does not mean that I have not experienced life-altering situations or that I am in a constant state of bliss. I still experience ups and downs as I would believe are normal. I will share one example where Choice Theory acted as my anchor. A little over six years ago I was hit on my motorcycle while coming home from work. This accident left me in the hospital for over 64 days, multiple surgeries, skin graphs, rehabilitation, and a below knee amputee. This experience also exposed me to a world I never knew and brought me a new perspective on living life. There is a colloquial saying, "you only live once" to that I disagree wholeheartedly. It is more accurate to say, "You only die once however, you get to live every day and how you live is your choice."

Choice Theory Reflections

Ellery is a happy man. He has chosen to live his life giving service to others as a counselor and a mentor. He has chosen a life of purpose and with that choice he is making himself happy. As a below knee amputee he certainly qualified for a reason to be unhappy but as he said, "Choice Theory acted as my anchor".

Is Ellery happy all the time? No, he, like all of us, said he experiences ups and downs. That is quite normal. Choice Theory doesn't promise you will be happy all the time. As a matter of fact, sometimes we choose to be unhappy and that's okay. The difference is, with understanding Choice Theory, we know why we are unhappy and we know there are things we can do to make ourselves happy again. We can make other choices. Ellery chose not to focus, in what he wrote, on his tragic accident and all the suffering he had to go through. He chose to reframe the experience to the positive. He is alive and he chooses to celebrate life. Recently, a new life he has chosen for himself is called married life. How fortunate for his wife to have married a happy man with Choice Theory in his pocket.

A Choice Theory Take Away:

What is the meaning of life? That question has been asked by erudite people the world over since time began. I doubt if anyone has come up with an answer to the question that everyone would agree upon.

What most people would agree upon is that we are alive through no choice of our own. Now that we are among the living, we get to make choices about how we live our lives.

How's that been going for you? If your answer is, "not so good", this story by Ellery Holesapple is just for you. Read every word of it again and ask, "What does my life mean"? Your answer has a lot to do with your present happiness.

10. Against All Odds, Choosing Happiness

Rose-Inza Kim

Well, I had to think hard how and when I was happy..There are so many small happy memories though...Actually I had a good happy life as a whole. It does not mean that I had no difficulties in trying to get what I wanted. Somehow I learned how to handle obstacles from my parents and from my grand-mother and not get discouraged with the results I got. Now I sometimes think I was born to live the way people do, who believe in Glasser's Choice Theory.

As I was entering primary school and then high school all I wanted seemed to be about surviving the Korean War. Then after that passed I turned my hopes toward my higher education. Before long I realized happiness because I had graduated from University in the United States, met the most wonderful man to marry and had 4 daughters, all healthy of mind and body. They all were happy growing up and each of them found more happiness marrying nice men and having healthy children. Each of them now have professional jobs and are very successful.

I, for more than 60 years worked as a university professor and psychological counselor. This career was very fulfilling and still is since I continue to have professional work to do. I am so fortunate to have met Dr. William Glasser and learned his Reality Therapy and Choice Theory ideas. That made me richer in knowledge and built my confidence in helping others to help themselves become happier in their lives than ever before.

These days I am doing my best to try for the rest of my life to remember that, whenever and whatever I do, I am doing my best to help this world to become better in every way than before I was born. So, I always give my best. And most of all I have God on my side. How could I not say that "I am happy and had a happy life. All this is possible because YOU ALL are here in my life space with me at this specific time and place. This is a MIRACLE!! Why now, why young me, why here ? Together, let's all choose to be HAPPY.

Choice Theory Reflections

Rose is a very special woman. She has expressed her joy and enthusiasm for a life well lived. Growing up in South Korea, during the Korean War must have been a huge challenge to her need for survival. Fear was pervasive and as a young child potentially devastating. But Rose is a formidable example of strength and the power of a very specific Quality World. She wanted, pursued and got her basic needs met. By nature of her genetic instructions to survive, to love and belong, to be powerful, to be free and to have the fun of always learning something new and useful she put the most need satisfying pictures to fulfill these needs in her Quality World. Every behavior she chose then was driven by these pictures to accomplish her goals, dreams and desires.

The accomplishments she achieved in her lifetime are so remarkable and many, it would take volumes to list them all. One example is she organized a comprehensive   training program to teach Glasser's Reality Therapy and Choice Theory to thousands of Koreans. She created and managed a large organization called the William Glasser Institute, Korea which conducts training programs and large worldwide conferences. Her impact has been felt in Korean life for over 40 years and is still being felt even today in the face of the North Korean global threat. Rose continues to teach people how to create happiness within their own lives, in spite of the turmoil of the external control world.

A Choice Theory Take Away

You can follow Rose's example and allow yourself to be inspired by what she has accomplished by living a Choice Theory life. Learning Choice Theory is easy. Integrating it into your life is the real challenge. We all live in a world where the pervasive belief is that people can control one another. If you are unhappy it is probably because you are trying to control or believe you are being controlled by other people. You spend a lot of time being   frustrated. Knowing and using Choice Theory will lead you to take charge of the only person in the world whose behavior you can control, your own.   No matter how much external control the world offered Rose, she prevailed and is a happy person because of the effective choices she made in her lifetime.

11. Natural Knowing

Julian Goldstein

You have asked me to define happiness and my answer is as follows: Happiness IS.

I find no reason to define happiness because it just IS. There is no doing ness to happiness because I can be happy by doing something, someone else doing something or me or anyone else doing nothing at all.

If you see a flower and your brain tells you that this is the most beautiful flower you have ever seen and your brain tells you that you are very happy to have had this experience, what good would it then do you to spend the next five minutes or five hours trying to figure out why or why not this is the most beautiful flower you have ever seen?

Let's play my game of happiness IS. I will go first.

Happiness is vanilla ice cream. You can pick your own flavor which now introduces you to the fact that choosing plays an important part in happiness.
Happiness is your fifth year birthday party for which your mother purchased an ice cream cake.
Happiness is the third time you went roller skating and never fell down.

Happiness is the first time you saw snow and got to play in it.

Happiness is the first kiss on your first date.

Happiness is eating your first hot dog at your first baseball game.

Happiness is horseback riding.

Happiness is getting into the college that was your first choice.

Happiness is fishing.

Happiness is having a best friend for life.

Happiness is having a healthy baby.

Happiness is finding a taxi on a rainy day.

Happiness is learning to tie your shoe laces.

By now, it should be obvious to you that, in a matter of a few minutes, I can run off another fifty items of what Happiness IS or has been to me. So now, you play my game and run off a list of ten or twenty of your life time experiences that make you happy. This is clearly a very easy game to play because, even in the course of a single day, or throughout our lifetimes, millions of experiences have or do make us happy without much effort on our part.

In fact, I believe that all of us are drama queens who specialize in noting all of the things that make us unhappy, upset or angry throughout the course of a day, while we choose to remain oblivious to the many experiences, both small and large, which make us smile, laugh or just feel happy for a few seconds or a few minutes each and every day.

As an Emergency Medical Technician I was taught about the fight or flight mechanism which is ingrained in each of us. I believe the same is true for happy and unhappy. I was not taught by my parents or my educators as to when I should or should not feel happy. I believe in what I call "Natural Knowing" and I believe that knowing when to be happy and when not to be happy is a gift delivered to me by my brain without the need for any education on the subject.

In proof of what I have just proposed as natural knowing I present the following: I am standing beside a crib in which there is a four month old baby with no discernible expression on its cute face. I now produce a baby rattle which I shake near the baby who now produces a delighted toothless smile. Can we all agree that the baby is happy? Who or what taught this baby to be happy at the sound of a rattle? I believe that it comes from the brain as natural knowing.

I believe that as we grow older and our brain is filled with billions of our experiences, the brain has memorized our reactions to these past experiences and will then immediately inform all parts of the body which need to know which emotion to display. Yes, we have choice and we have told our brain many times over what our choice is and why. The brain never forgets and the message is sent . Lips, open and display teeth in a smile, says the brain, and we are happy.

Choice Theory Reflections

In his example of experiencing what his brain tells him is the most beautiful flower he has ever seen,

Julian gives a perfect example of a Quality World picture.

The flower he sees matches perfectly what he wants in his quality world so there is no need to do anything about changing what he wants or what he has. Happiness IS, in this case, effortless. Would that all of life could be that easy!

In Julian's game of Happiness IS, he lists very clearly in visual language some of the pictures he has stored over many years in his Quality World. He invites us to play his game and list the need satisfying pictures that we see in our own Quality Worlds. This is such a good idea! Happiness relies on us, at any given point, to know what we really want.

Julian points out, in a very astute observation that, we often choose to focus on the unhappinesses in our lives that feel painful. This is an example of getting stuck, even if only momentarily, in the back wheels of the Total Behavior car, painful feelings and physiology. We do have the choice to focus on our front wheels instead and choose the acting and thinking which could take us in a happier direction. Not an easy task because when our back wheels are stuck in unhappiness, our whole car is often immobilized.

When Julian points out that we are not taught to be happy or sad by our parents or teachers, he accurately describes this phenomena as Natural Knowing. In Choice Theory language, Natural Knowing is the genetic instructions we all receive, which Glasser calls, our internal motivation to satisfy Basic Needs. We then, naturally know, instantly, if our needs are being satisfied or not. It is because of this knowledge that we put our very own specific pictures, based on each need into our Quality Worlds. These pictures motivate everything we do.

Why did the four month old baby in the crib smile when Julian shook the baby rattle? Most people would say because he shook the rattle. Choice Theory teaches that all of us are internally motivated, not externally motivated to behave. The baby was born with the need for love and belonging. This means that the person holding the rattle, not the rattle alone, satisfied the baby's needs for admiration, attention, recognition, being included and having fun. The holder of the rattle had begun the process of connecting with the baby in a need satisfying relationship. The baby has a natural knowing about having need satisfying relationships and will attempt to have them for the rest of his or her life.

A Choice Theory Take Away

If we connect with ourselves by understanding what we need and connect with the people we want to have in our lives by understanding what they need, happiness comes naturally. No one teaches us to be happy. How true! As Julian so aptly puts it, "knowing when to be happy and when not to be happy is a gift delivered to me by my brain." It is a gift because it gives us reliable signals, the pleasure or pain experienced when basic needs are being met or not. Follow your natural knowing signals and choose behaviors that bring you closer to knowing yourself and that have the best chance of connecting you with the people you want in your life.

A good question to ask yourself every morning when you wake up is, What shall I choose to do today that will help me fulfill my need for Love and Belonging? Power? Freedom? Fun? and of course, Survival? Start with a good breakfast and look for somebody who wants a hug.

Did you know that hugging benefits your health? Hugging increases the "happiness hormone", oxytocin, which is good for heart health and reduces the harmful physical effects of stress, including its impact on your blood pressure and heart rate. Hugs can also fight infections and boost your immune system. One of the simplest ways to meet your need for Love and Belonging is with a hug. And remember, a hug is as beneficial to the giver as it is to the receiver.

U.C.L.A. Hospital gives all open-heart surgery patients a Huggy Bear to squeeze against their chest to protect the incision when they have to cough. You can imagine how therapeutic hugging this bear can be. Here's an idea. Become a Huggy Bear. A lot of people in this uncertain world we live in could sure use a big hug right now.

12. Happiness Simple

Everne Spiegel

Happiness is many things to many people. It goes hand in hand with good health, good family relationships and your individual ability to cope with adversity most of the time. It is attached to events such as the birth of a child, listening to great music, smelling night blooming Jasmine on a Summer evening. Happiness is a grandchild's kiss, a new puppy's exuberance and best of all, the love and support of a wonderful family. Most important to me is the trust, loving companionship and respect of my dear husband.

Choice Theory Reflections

Sometimes it is the simplest of experiences that bring you in touch with your own personal source of happiness. Not once did Everne mention money or power in her description of happiness. She obviously has a very high need for not only getting her need for love and belonging met, but she also has a high need for giving her love to all those around her.

Everne, is one of those rare and fortunate beings who were born to a life filled with giving and loving. One can see it in her face with its warm, inviting expressions. And what she often gets in return is the love and caring from all those who know her. She is the essence of happiness.

In Choice Theory we teach people to ask themselves one simple question if they want to be happy most of the time. Always ask yourself, "If I say or do this will it bring me closer to the ones I want in my life or drive us further apart? Happy people, like Everne, always choose to do what will preserve their relationships and keep them connected to the people they care about.

A Choice Theory Take Away

The reason we feel unhappy when we are disconnected is because we all have been genetically programed to satisfy our needs for love and belonging. When we are not getting enough of these needs met we experience the pain of loneliness or sensory deprivation. If you are experiencing any such feelings, this is an emergency. Call someone who knows you and tell them what you are experiencing. Just another human being's voice on the phone could be a beginning point for a connection. Make this choice. Take this step to connect. Remember everyone has the same need as you do, to love and be loved, to belong and to connect. They need you as much as you need them.

13. Yes Sir, That's My Baby

Roger Samuel

I've been witness to many amazing sights in my life, so many of them related to my travels in remote places. I've looked into the eyes of the woman I loved and knew it would be forever. When I ask myself, though, what sight stands out above all the others, I have no doubt about my response.

It was near the end of my second year in dental school, and Gail and I lived in married students housing in San Francisco. Between the savings we had from before we were married, Gail working in the personnel office of the university, me working in labs at night after school and the availability of student loans, there was no question that we could afford for me to finish school. Near the end of the semester in June, Gail stopped taking birth control pills.

Letting our parents know that they were going to become grandparents was one of the best parts of sharing the news. It was easy to tell Gail's parents, since they were also visiting Philadelphia at the time. My parents required a phone call, and while we kidded around at the start of the call, my father said "Mollie, I think they're trying to tell us that Gail is pregnant."

When we were back in San Francisco and the new semester had started, Gail went to the medical center to be seen in the obstetrics clinic. Since it was a teaching institution we were also assigned a post-graduate nursing student (Marcia Petrini) who visited us regularly to evaluate how we were doing. We watched films and took training on natural childbirth and because I was a dental student they said that I could be present for the delivery, something not commonplace at the time, but we both wanted very much. It was also comforting to know that Marcia would go through the delivery with us.

Gail did really well and continued to work until three weeks before she was due. Marcia became an integral part of our lives, and the information she passed on about pregnancy, childbirth and infant care was so helpful. We got the apartment ready, felt the baby move, picked out a name (one male, one female) and just counted down the days.

We went to bed on the night of April 4th, and Gail had started to feel something before we went to bed. She didn't say anything, but at about eleven she woke me. She remembers me jumping out of bed and into my pants in the blink of an eye. We called Marcia, and, as instructed, drove down the hill to the hospital at about 5:30 in the morning.

Marcia met us and helped with checking Gail in, and then the three of us stayed in the room talking, playing cards and pausing only for the regular contractions. And we waited while Gail worked.

And worked. And worked. There is a very good reason why it's called labor.

With all of the excitement and the doctor yelling at Gail to push and bear down, the baby came. She was crying before she was out. We still didn't know if it was a boy or girl. And then there she was. The miracle had happened. It was over and she was perfect. What relief and joy I felt!

Poor Gail was tired and hungry, but the kitchen was closed and all they had was tomato soup and a sandwich of undetermined origin. Gail hates tomato soup. We decided I would go across the street to eat and bring something back for her.

As I sat in the restaurant waiting for my hamburger and fries, I was overwhelmed by what had happened. In the silence that followed my tumultuous day I was struck, in a way I hadn't been previously, by the fact that there was now a new person in the world for whom I would have a lifetime of responsibility. When I got back to Gail with something to eat, all I could do was marvel at each of them. And so it has always been.

Choice Theory Reflections

What a beautiful entry-into-fatherhood story! The awe and gratefulness that Roger expressed is what life giving life is all about. In Choice Theory terms, we are all driven by our need for Survival, which includes, the reproduction of the species. The joy and satisfaction we feel when our new baby is born seems far removed from the survival of the species need. The need to survive is an old brain function. Having a baby of your very own surely fulfills new brain needs as well, which are psychological and just as necessary for survival. Just think of the love and belonging, the powerful pride, the choices that you freely make and the joy you feel getting to know and understand your new infant. Your child's survival is now part of your own motivation to survive. Your child will carry your genes into the future for generations to come.

A Choice Theory Take Away

New parents would benefit greatly by learning Choice Theory. Understanding human behavior before the baby is born can help the new parents cope with the many challenges that are sure to arrive with the new arrival. What comes built in to the child are his or her own set of basic needs. Very soon, almost immediately, the baby begins to create a personal Quality World and starts to put specific pictures in it that might satisfy those basic needs.

When baby begins to cry, Choice Theory knowledgeable parents know that baby wants some need satisfied. Does baby want cuddles (love and belonging) or maybe baby is just hungry (survival)? When baby screams, is it pain (survival) or anger (power) driven?

Baby begins to create a Quality World made up of pictures of the most need satisfying people he or she has experienced since birth. The person caring for baby is usually the first picture to be entered in baby's Quality World and most likely will remain for the child's whole lifetime. Similarly, in the animal kingdom this is called imprinting. Parents who are placed by their child in the child's Quality World bond well and have the most influence on their child's choices in life. Good Choice Theory advise for parents to remember is, take care to nurture your relationship with your children.

A few months before he died, Dr.Glasser wisely said about parenting, "Treat your children as if they are good and always do things WITH them in which they can succeed".

14. Do You Believe in Magic?

Billie Fischer

Columbus, Georgia in our studio apartment, my newly single mom and I lived. She got the pull-out couch and I slept in the closet on a crib mattress suspended between two shelving units.Admittedly it was not a tiny closet and it suited my five year old self.

I do not remember much from that time. Mother worked as a buyer at a department store and I went to school I suppose. We had no friends or at least I didn't. We had left my beloved grandmother, aunt and uncle, my cousins, not to mention my biological father and his parents back in Illinois. I still sucked my thumb.

One day I got a loose tooth and I had heard a rumor about a tooth fairy. What was that all about? Eventually my tooth fell out and I prepared for the coming of the tooth fairy. That night I took my bath, put on my prettiest nightgown, carefully put my tooth under my pillow, said my prayers (loudly so that the tooth fairy would take notice) and went to sleep.

That morning, buzzing with anticipation, I quickly looked under my pillow. Whaaatt?There was nothing there. Nothing. I jumped off my mattress and headed for our kitchenette where Mother was preparing eggs, toast, and the dreaded cod liver oil pill that she made me take every morning. "Mother, Mother (she insisted that I call her Mother) I put my tooth under my pillow and she didn't come. The tooth fairy didn't come!"

My mother looked puzzled but then she knelt down and said, "Billie Jean, did you hear that?"

I listened and I swear to this day, I heard something . . . a tinkly, tinkly sound. Tinkly, tinkly. I rushed to my closet bedroom, picked up my pillow again and there it was! A shiny quarter! Now that was happiness and even more than happiness, it was when I was truly convinced that there was magic in this world.

Choice Theory Reflection

Billie Jean had placed the idea a tooth fairy in her Quality World and at that moment she began to expect something wonderful to happen to her. Her creative system was activated and her brain took over producing a tinkly sound that she actually heard as if it were real. It is truly like magic. Ask any composer about the sounds his or her brain creates and magically are heard as a melody for a new song. Ask any artist what is seen in his or her brain while painting images on canvas to become a great work of art.

Having a Quality World full of sounds and images that we hear and see is the magic we are capable of creating at will anytime or anywhere in an attempt to get what we want. I knew someone who wanted something so much that she not only had a clear picture of it in her head but she actually wrote it down on paper and posted it on her refrigerator as a reminder. Many months after the posted note had fallen off by itself my friend got exactly what she wanted. Is this magic? Yes, and no. Yes, because your Quality World is a magical place for storing your dreams. No, it's not magic because, unbeknownst to us, our creative system is constantly working to help us create the behaviors needed to get us where we have to be when our dreams are about to come true.

A Choice Theory Take Away

If you want to experience magic, become aware of what you really want. Visualize it. Talk about it. Evaluate it. Ask yourself if it is truly what you want. Clarify your picture by sorting out the details. Then let it be. Let your creative system take over. It is fully functioning day and night, even though you are unaware of it. When it offers you a direction to take or a new idea to try, pay attention. But most of the time you will just go on living your life and then one day, as if by magic there you have it. Your tooth fairy comes and you are in wonder at the magic of it all.

15. If You're Happy and You Know It

Steve Wallace

It has been said that 'Love is never having to say you're sorry' Being Happy is never having to say you're happy. To me being happy when as a child I knew my parents were always there for me and remained so till they passed.

Happy:
Visiting Grandma O'Hagan and being embraced by the aroma of her freshly baked Soda Bread
Visiting Grandma Wallace and being embraced by the aroma of her freshly baked Lemon Cake
My Mother, Grandma Wallace and Grandma O'Hagan preparing the Thanksgiving and Christmas feasts
Realizing that my pesky sisters had pretty girlfriends
Rebuilding my first car engine with my buddy Ed and it actually worked
Vietnam...
Getting a Care Package while in Vietnam from my Mother with: Birthday balloons, banners, candles and a cake – that was as hard as concrete (we soaked it in beer and was just fine)
Letters from home
Realizing that I was still alive...

Coming home after three years serving overseas and having my youngest sister tug on my sleeve and ask me if I was her brother
Meeting Shearon
Still being Alive…

Choice Theory Reflections

Steve's happy memories are filled with his wonderful Quality World pictures. Remembering specific pictures from the past is one way to become aware of feelings of happiness in the present. Conversely, remembering painful experiences from the past can perpetuate feelings of unhappiness in the present.

Dr. Glasser strongly emphasized the importance of focusing on the present because you cannot change what happened in the past. But remembering the past successes and happinesses of your life can be extremely need satisfying. The older we get the more memories we have to share. If you ask any senior citizens to tell you memories they particularly enjoyed, they will regale you with some pretty good stories. This is a great way to connect and meet your and their need for love and belonging.

Many years ago I was a High School Counselor and ran a leadership training program for the students in the school who were identified as non-traditional leaders. Instead of running for office in the Student Counsel, they were more likely to run an underground numbers racket in the school basement. My job was to redirect their efforts to more constructive projects. Once they realized I was putting them in charge of making some significant changes in their environment, they got on board.

I first sat them down in a circle and asked them one question. If you had the chance, what changes would you make in this community? Immediately , I was hit with a barrage of complaints. There's nothing for teenagers to do here except break curfew and get in trouble. This was the basic problem because it was absolutely true. I asked, "Would you like to change that?" With a skeptical look on their collective faces they all answered, "Yes."

One of the many projects they did, that is relevant here, came about because of dissension and even anger, between the teens and the senior citizens who were supposed to share space in the newly opened Library and adjoining Senior Citizen Center. Both groups were unhappy with each other and resented the mere presence of the other in the space.

I asked the students if they had grandparents. Surprisingly, I was told for various reasons, most of them were not involved with their grandparents. We discussed that and they decided having grandparents might be okay. I asked, "So, what if you asked the principal if you could invite some senior citizens from the Center to our school to have lunch with you?"   That lunch turned into a planning session, involving the students and an equal number of seniors citizens, who started The Taylor High School Adopt a Grandparent Program.

The students were very interested in what life was like when their adopted grandparent was their age. That grew into supplying the teens with tape recorders to interview their "grandparents" and create a living history for them to have as a gift for their own children. The teens who participated in this project grew personally and the community became friendlier. The teenagers, especially, perceived themselves differently and that had a lasting effect on their lives.

A Choice Theory Take Away

It is never too late to connect and build relationships. Ask yourself who you know or who you would like to know, right now, to share happy memories with.   Steve described how important it was and is to him, having someone there for him. Maybe choosing to be there for someone, just to listen to their stories, could be one of the most need satisfying things you ever do.

16. And That's What Friends Are For

Maria Lee

We grew up poor in the Midwest. That wasn't the happy memory, it just made getting gifts more memorable.We were given gifts two times a year, at Christmas and our birthday. The gifts were usually quite useful. We were given beautiful new sweaters and wool coats for the brutal winters, shiny patent leather shoes with bows, and sometimes party dresses with layers and layers of petticoats.

One year was especially grand. I am not sure, now that I am looking back, if it was because I had broken my leg, or because I had plenty of clothes. I was the middle of three girls in my family and scrawny. Back then skinny was not cool. And so I would have my older sister's clothes passed down to me and my younger sisters clothes passed up to me. I had plenty to wear in the fashionable neighborhood outside Detroit.

It was 1961, I was 10, and Christmas was drawing near. Both my parents worked then and it seemed there was more for us. Earlier that summer we took our first family vacation since arriving in America. We went to Pennsylvania to visit our old neighbors from Italy. I remember my older sister having her first real crush on Tony, the family's oldest son. I had a crush on him too, but I was not a teenager, not even close.

I went shopping with my mom that holiday season to help pick out presents for our cousins. I saw the most beautiful doll I had ever seen. Why, she was at least three feet tall and had beautiful blue eyes that opened and closed and curly blonde hair and she could stand. I can see her in my mind's eye as if it were yesterday. Mamma noticed me admiring her. She said it was too expensive and I never gave it another thought. Well, maybe? That year, my present wasn't underneath the tree, because I would have guessed it. When Mamma came from the basement with that three foot box, my heart skipped a beat. I knew. And there she was my first, new baby doll. She had various names throughout the year and she could even wear the dress I wore in Italy when I was three. I did not "outgrow" her until I was thirteen. She lived in the basement, many years after.

Oh, and my best friend Connie, in junior high had beautiful blue eyes and curly blonde hair. It is almost as if my doll had come to life. Amazing, now I am back in Italy, writing this happy memory and getting it to you in an instant, so many years later. This memory brought on so much emotion I cried while writing it. Connie passed away from cancer in her forties. She had lived on the corner of the street near our house. She was so American and she was my first real friend outside the family.

Choice Theory Reflections

Friendship is precisely one of the best examples of Choice Theory you can find. No one will disagree that having a friend is a choice two people make to be inclusive with one another. Our need for love and belonging is a powerful motivator for developing friendships. The sense of belonging we feel when a friend is there for us is incredibly need satisfying.

Maria, remembers her friend Connie, when she was writing about a favorite Christmas present she received over 50 years ago. Connie had a permanent place in Maria's Quality World. Tears flowed from Maria's eyes remembering that doll and how much she reminded her of her best friend, Connie, from so long ago.

A Choice Theory Take Away

There are certain ways we treat our friends. We use Choice Theory, and almost never use External Control. When asked why we never try to control our friends, people have said to Dr. Glasser, "Why, we'd lose them!" Dr. Glasser suggests that we treat our family members and the people closest to us in the same manner. When people get married and have children, often the element of ownership enters into the equation and with the perception of ownership comes the need to control the persons closest to us. A lot of unhappiness ensues from failing to treat our relatives and spouses with Choice Theory in mind. External Control always destroys relationships.

17. Your Life Your Choice

Brian Lennon

Let's face it! We men are afraid to be happy! We call it contentment, a lesser state and one that is safer to aspire to for fear the evil eye or some other malefactor will gloat over our failure to achieve full happiness. Setting aside such misgivings and as a massive fan of Choice Theory I was keen to find out how on earth happiness might fit in. I got the idea that a quick analysis of unhappiness could be a good starting point.

Choice Theory teaches that we all have basic needs but each of us develops a set of "pictures", of ways to meet our needs. We then activate those pictures attempting to make them happen in the real world through our behavior. If then, meeting all our needs is happiness, how and where can things go wrong?

Obviously if I have very few pictures in my Quality World, I'm off to a bad start. At a very basic level, if I know of only one activity for a rainy day then I'm more likely to be miserable when the rain comes.

Then again I might have lots of pictures but simply not know how to convert these into behaviors. For example, I know that joining a club would enhance my social life but I am shy and cannot bring myself to go through that door.

I might have pictures that I can achieve easily but they are not really effective need-satisfiers. They are ineffective pictures. For example, I could drink myself silly rather easily. For a short while I would be quite merry but that wears off leaving me with a hang-over and, worse still, possibly an addiction and health issues. The picture didn't quite live up to its promises.

Another sure-fire way to achieve unhappiness would be to expect happiness to come from outside of myself, from a bottle or a pill or, heavens above, from politicians. Choice Theory is all about internal control and to rely on an external control solution would be risky. If I rely on an external control view of my life then I lessen my chances of meeting my needs.

So, where do we go from there? What did my quick trip through unhappiness teach me about happiness itself? Well, in the first place I need to enrich my world of pictures and I can only do that by trying new activities, meeting new people or reading about how to improve my life. Trying new experiences can improve my chances of achieving happiness.

As for pictures that I find hard to activate as behaviors, there are obviously a whole range of personal skills I need to acquire: relationship skills, assertiveness, problem-solving, decision-making, planning, time-management. At some point in my life I need to learn not to be put off by the initial difficulty I experience in new undertakings. I need to take the serenity prayer to heart, the serenity to accept what I cannot change, the courage to change what I can and the wisdom to know the difference. Yes, indeed, serenity, courage and wisdom! One of the things I can change is ignorance. When I do not know how to do something I can decide to learn about it, to get information from others … or I could choose to sit in the dark!

To offset the attractiveness of ineffective pictures such as drugs, I need to experience truly need-satisfying pictures and that links to the earlier points, the need to try out a host of different experiences, to relish the company of inspirational people, to learn effective coping skills, to seek need satisfaction in a pro-active way.

As for relying on external sources for my happiness, I need the Choice Theory attitudes. I need to know that whatever my next step in life is, it starts with me. It starts from where I am because I cannot start from anywhere else. I need to learn that my feelings, even the negative ones of anger, frustration and depression are all my friends because they alert me to problems. They are not diseases or disorders that invade my system but are well-functioning signals telling me that something has gone wrong and, the bit we forget about, they tell me to fix it. They are painful because that is how they remind us that all is not well, and they become more painful if we do not heed these signals.

Reflecting on my own life, I believe that my happiness has indeed relied on a series of important attitudes: openness to new experiences, contact with inspirational people, being pro-active about situations I did not like, a willingness to learn what I needed to know and valuing the wonderful relationships that have lit up my life.

In my own life I remember the moments …

- I remember the love of my parents who sheltered me as they encouraged me to try new experiences;
- the teachers who shared the wonderment of their learning;
- the shopkeeper who taught me about decimals and the more important lesson that we can learn almost anything from almost anybody;
- the day I got fed up with my own shyness and decided to fix it for once and for all;
- the moment I realized I could learn whatever I wanted to learn when I heard that the human brain has more tetra-bytes of storage than any lifetime could fill;
- the afternoon the tide left my boat high and dry on the sand and I learned that even if some things were beyond my control it did not mean the end of my happiness;
- the morning I first heard Bill Glasser and how his ideas made so much sense of my life;
- the day, every day, that the love of my wife teaches me that life is precious.

Choice Theory Reflections

Brian's explanation of unhappiness and happiness is an exceedingly accurate overview of Dr. Glasser's ideas. In Brian's description of how to be unhappy, he gives examples of ways people choose external control to destroy their relationships and create unhappiness in their lives. His is a very effective contrast between Choice Theory and External Control and in reading what Brian wrote over again you will find ideas for applying the information to choices you are currently making today that result in happiness or in the unhappiness you feel.

A Choice Theory Take Away

If you are unhappy here are some things to do that could help you.

First, Examine your Quality World and determine if any of the pictures of what you want are unrealistic. For example, if you are dating someone who does not have marriage in their Quality World and you desperately want to marry that person, in Choice Theory terms what would you do? Could you consider taking that person out of your Quality World and replacing them with a more realistic picture?

Next, If you are not finding a match, in the Real World, for a picture you desire in your Quality World, consider changing the only things you can control, what you want or what you are doing to get what you want.

Finally, ask yourself this question: Is what I am choosing to do now helping me get what I want or, based on what I have learned about Choice Theory, is my behavior hurting my chances of me getting what I really want? What you choose to do will determine how happy or unhappy you make yourself.

18. It Must Be Good To Be You

Mark Thompson

I am usually caught up in the details of the here and now. I allow my life to be one big to-do list. I have a brief celebration every time I cross something off. When something pops up unexpectedly and I complete it, I will actually write it on my list just so I can cross it off. What's on my mind on the drive home is everything that's still sitting on my list waiting for me the next day.

Nailing a task or initiative gives me a rush like no other. The more challenging or seemingly impossible the task, the more I crave it. That could be why my college asked me to lead the creation of a new bachelor's degree program for secondary education. I am excited beyond words at the thought of training the next generation of teachers who will work in the schools that serve our communities.

The date for our inaugural meeting races toward me, the pressure mounts, and I get caught up in the details of the here and now. Some things are going right, but many things seem to be going wrong or taking longer than they should. I planned to go home early the day before so I can get plenty of rest for the next day, but it's very late at night when I finally pull into my driveway.

The following morning my friend Claudia sits down next to me. "I just met your wife," she says. "She's your biggest fan! You have a lot of people who care about you. It must be good to be you." Her statement shocks me. I feel exposed and unsure of what to say. This person has just been assessing my life in a way that I myself have not.

I feel sorry for her because I have clearly duped her. She doesn't see my life in its entirety as I do; my failed initiatives, failed marriages, loved ones so far away it hurts me every day, other loved ones I'm glad to be far away from, my tendency to hold grudges, my vanity…. Speaking of the latter, my weight, proliferating wrinkles, and thinning hair must have escaped her notice. "Um, thank you," I mutter. "I'm more fortunate than I should be."

We go back to work. I look down at my laptop, but I'm really just staring at the screen trying to process what she said. Is it good to be me? No! It would be good to be George Clooney. It would be great to be Peter Branson!

Snapped out of the to-do's of the here and now, I begin looking at the people around the room, starting with Claudia. This meeting was only possible because of her many hours of hard work. She has offered me her confidence and friendship which she doesn't offer to everyone.

At another table, I see a man who could easily run his own college, but humbly serves in a position for which he is overqualified, and patiently tutors me in the processes of higher education. I see my best friend who went to the print shop with me just to keep me company, and gave me hours of time helping prepare the name tents and materials. I see the woman I love more than I love breathing, who every day re-earns my respect, exhilarates me, and is an epic classroom teacher. I see my mentor who undertook a 4-hour round trip just because her being there was important to me. I see new friends I met only that morning now throwing themselves into this work because they, too, hear the calling. I think of my boss who has faith I can pull this off and be a good steward of our college's reputation.

In a Mr. Holland's Opus-type moment, I see twenty-five years of my life has converged into a single room in the form of people, and personal and professional relationships. Everyone is putting hands on work to create something important that will outlast us. That's when it hits me.

I am loved and cared for; I have been given friendship from people who are judicious in handing it out; I am vain; my wife is my biggest fan; separations hurt because I have people in my life I love; I have mentors; I have tutors; I hold grudges; I am trusted by my colleagues; I exacerbate the idiosyncrasies of others for my own amusement; I am surrounded by people daily I look forward to seeing; I am trying to be a better person; and…

…I am happy. I guess it is good to be me.

Choice Theory Reflections

Mark is a man, who is who he wants to be. This is what living a Choice Theory life is all about. Mark has chosen to live his life in the present with a purpose. People like Mark are a gift to the world because they get things done that help other people besides themselves. He has a high need for love and belonging.

Writing to do lists is a sure sign of a high need for power. Choice Theory explains the need for Power as manifested in two forms of behavior. There is the external control kind of power, which is forceful power over everything and everyone and there is the intrinsic reward kind of power that is satisfied within ourselves by our accomplishments. We all tend to have both kinds of these power needs driving us at any given time, but Choice Theory is all about internal control and self-empowerment.

Mark has a very high need for the achievements kind of internal power. He is a great leader because people believe in him and his purpose so they choose to follow him and implement his ideas. Why do they want to follow his leadership? People have an uncanny sense of what is or will eventually become need satisfying for them. That is why great leaders succeed and accomplish all they do. People are internally motivated to follow their lead.

One of the pitfalls of a high need for power is the tendency for self-criticism or self-doubt. The urge to be perfect can, and often does, put a damper on happiness, especially in the internally motivated, high achiever. Mark like most people wants to be his best self. Whenever he allows himself to admit, "I guess it is good to be me." He will realize more personal happiness.

A Choice Theory Take Away

Do you feel like it is good to be you? Early in his practice, Dr. Glasser worked as a Psychiatrist at an orthopedic hospital for paraplegic and quadriplegic patients in Los Angeles. It was a very challenging position because, often he heard patients say, "Just kill me Doc. What have I got to live for?" Dr. Glasser could, of course, understand their pain and hopelessness. He began to dread going to work, sometimes feeling practically useless.

Then one morning he decided to ask the patients a new question. Instead of asking them the usual, "How do you feel today?" He asked them what they were going to do for someone else today. Well, this question caused quite an angry uproar. Outraged, the patients yelled "What do you mean? How dare you talk to us like that?" To that outcry Dr. Glasser said to one man, "Look you have two eyes that work, you have no legs but you have two hands, can you read?" The man said, "Yes". Dr. Glasser said, "See that guy over there? He can't see and even if he could he can't hold a book with no hands. Do you think you could read the newspaper to him?"

"Yes, I think I can," said the man. This started a completely different set of total behaviors on the ward. Many of the patients began a new life that day and eventually came to believe, "I guess it is good to be me."

In Chapter 9 you read about Ellery Holsapple, who has chosen a life of service to others as his purpose. He focuses on what he can do, not what he can't do and his life is full of happiness. Find one thing important to you that could give your life purpose and do it with all your heart.

19. What Goes Around Comes Around

RoxAnne Triché

As a young parent who finally got a child through high school and talking about college, it shocked me to discover I was pregnant. The thought of raising another child, just when I got one child with one foot out the door, was not something I expected to do in my mid-thirties.

Finally, my second child was born, the first few years progressed rather smoothly (until she began talking and thinking on their own). As she left elementary school, they placed her in the Gifted and Talented Education Program (GATE). Unfortunately, as time went on, you could imagine my surprise when she failed ALL her classes, including P.E. By the time she entered high school our relationship had hit every low possible. I was convinced, I would be featured on the TV show America's Most Wanted and she would be featured on Unsolved Mysteries. That's how much we were at odds with one another. I can honestly say it was the most frustrating time in our relationship.

I often wondered what happened, what could I have possibly done wrong with this child? Why is it she consciously failed every class... going from the GATE program to remedial classes? How does this happen? What did I miss? Where did I go wrong? Am I that bad of a parent I can't get my child through school?

Finally, I concluded it was all her fault; she was trying to break me; she hated me, all she wanted was to make my life miserable. I believed she wanted me to give her my attention every minute of every day and never have a life of my own. I was anxious, in my late forties and wanted to be like other's my age. Unfortunately, she was making it impossible for me; she would never let me go, she wanted me to be at her every beck and call, and still, she was failing all her classes.

We were at the point where we did not want to see each other. I dreaded coming home. The thought of seeing her gave me anxiety, it was sad, as a parent, I did not want to see my own child. It was so bad; I become depressed when driving down our street, why, because I knew she would be there. Sad to say, I hated my life with her, I even considered asking her father, her godparents, our family, anyone to take her for a few months... or even longer.

Finally, one day, when I got home, I walked in; we went through our normal routine; "Is your homework done?" "NO" as she rolled her eyes and gave me every body sign she could muster to let me know she didn't want to talk. "Go to your room and get it done I'm adding six more years onto your already 45-year sentence of being grounded!" "Whatever" she goes upstairs and slams her door.

I remember sitting on the couch; looking up, and saying God, "what do you want me to do with your child?" Seriously, it immediately came to me, to call her down and ask her "what do you want from me?" God said, "Ask her to tell you how to parent her." WHAT? Are you kidding me? I'm the parent, I know what's best for this child (ha, how did that work out). After agonizing over it, I called her downstairs and asked; "What do you want from me? Where did I go wrong? What do you expect from me? Why do you hate me so much? What do you want in a mother? (I know I was only supposed to ask one question but... yeah.) She stared at me, I could still see it, she thought I was setting her up, she was hesitant to answer, but eventually did.

Long story short, we talked on and off for the next two days and ended up creating a "safe room," a room where we could say anything, we wanted to each other and the other person could not respond, judge, give advice, scold, react, nothing. In the "safe room" our only job was to listen, truly listen intending to hear the other person.

The point was to rebuild trust and respect so we could open the lines of communication with one other. Heck, we even created a buzz word (we did not create this word but used it as our buzz world) "supercalifragilisticexpialidocious." If one of us forgot the agreement (respecting each other) and displayed old habits, we would say this word to cause the other person to pause and regroup. It turned out to be the best turn around in a relationship I had experienced to date.

To this day, she and I can talk about any and everything, believe me, most parents are not ready to hear any and everything.   It's nice to know, she mimics this process with her now three-year-old child. When I saw that, all I could think of is "what goes around comes around." Hee, hee, I can't wait, to see how it all turns out.

roxanne@internalempowement.com

Choice Theory Reflections

RoxAnne describes how she practiced the most important tenant Choice Theory offers, "The only person's behavior you can control is your own!" By not using external control, thus building a need-satisfying relationship with her daughter, RoxAnne chose to make herself happy. Was it easy? Obviously, it was one of the hardest things she ever attempted to do with her daughter. It meant changing how she chose to communicate with her.

RoxAnne mentioned the importance of listening in the process of rebuilding her relationship with her skeptical daughter. We all have a need for power and one of the easiest ways we can fulfill our need for power is by being listened to by someone important to us. But that requires another person to do the listening. Ultimately it is a two way street, but RoxAnne took that road and was wildly successful. It is remarkable how effective listening is in trying to repair a relationship, especially with a teenager. In regard to teenagers, Glasser said, "When you stop controlling, you gain control."

The biggest pay off of all, besides getting along with her daughter and enjoying their relationship, is now seeing her granddaughter reap the benefits of having a Choice Theory Mother and Grandmother. RoxAnne is now Choice Theory/Reality Therapy Certified and having this experience with her daughter on board, she was certainly pre-qualified for successfully completing the certification process. She currently serves as Executive Vice President, IECAST, Inc.

A Choice Theory Take Away

Go back and look at the questions RoxAnne asked her daughter starting with , "What do you want from me?". Then ask yourself if you might be able to use any of these questions when speaking to someone with whom you are having difficulties. All it takes to mend a broken relationship is someone who is willing to give up the urge to control and become willing to listen, really listen to the other without judgement.

Dr. Glasser called this kind of practice "The Solving Circle". RoxAnne called it "A Safe Room". Basically, two or more people decide if they want a better relationship, they carefully listen to each other and then each state what they would be willing to do, beginning now, to improve the relationship. Success always depends on the belief that the only person's behavior you can control is your own.

To quote Dr. Glasser, Please consider his words when dealing with teenagers, "When you stop controlling, you gain control".

20. There Are No Quick Fixes

Shearon Bogdanovic

Like the old joke comparing being rich and poor: I have had both happiness and "depression": and believe me, happiness is better. Happiness seems to be a heightened sense of well being. When we are happy, it is possible to experience pleasure in everyday experiences, and joy when something special occurs. Before I knew about choice theory, happiness was a mystery - a surprise. Looking back, I notice that when I was happy, my life seemed well balanced. Work, home, and relationships were all in order. Looking back at the miserable times, I know I was depressing very hard. Usually my relationships were out of control, starting with problems at home or possibly problems at work.

Learning choice theory was quite possibly a life saver for me, because I learned how the perception of control is central to everyone's personal life. It took a lot of practice to realize the limits of my own ability to control. When I was able to focus on my personal reality and give up trying to "fix" myself and others, I noticed the misery dissipating. I notice the more I work to relinquish resentments, past slights, and other negative ideas, the happier I become. Even now, some days can be happier than others; and when I notice a low feeling, I know

I can rely on myself to choose behaviors compatible with happiness! I am so grateful!

Summary Comments

If you want to be happy and are not now experiencing it, re read Shearon's contribution above. She offers one of the most important concepts in Choice Theory, If you cannot give up the use of external control, don't anticipate the possibility of having happy relationships. Happy relationships are destroyed by External Control. True happiness is possible with good relationships. By knowing and using Choice Theory, you can improve all of your relationships. Shearon, as a CT/RT certified instructor, teaches Glasser's ideas effectively because she lives these ideas everyday in her personal life.

You may be asking, what advise would you give to people who want to make themselves happy? Here is a to-do list for you to consider:

1. Find somebody to love and remember, you don't own them.
2. Get a Dog if you want unconditional love. Or, if you're an optimist, get a cat.
3. Join a group that has a purpose you are passionate about.
4. Hang out with people who have a great sense of humor.
5. Look for the funny side of life and laugh out loud as often as you can.
6. Do something nice for another person, especially if you don't like them.

7. Don't put yourself down for what you haven't accomplished yet.
8. Reframe the negative to the positive.
9. Have strong convictions but be willing to learn more and negotiate differences.
10. Believe in Magic and then trust your creativity.

A Final Choice Theory Take Away

If you want to get rid of the harmful effects of external control in your life Dr. Glasser offers the following prescription: Stop using the seven deadly habits that define external control and destroy your happiness. They are, Criticizing, such as fault finding; Blaming, such as holding grudges; Complaining, such as a negative attitude about everything; Nagging, such as relentlessly repeating orders; Threatening such as warning of impending punishment, Punishing such as inflicting physical or emotional pain; and Rewarding to Control such as bribing. Ellery Holesapple explained these habits further in chapter 9.

If you want to be happy, Dr. Glasser recommends you replace these destructive habits with the caring habits of Choice Theory. They are: Supporting, such as being there for others in need; Encouraging, such as cheering on an effort; Listening, such as actually hearing someone; Accepting, such as realizing and celebrating differences; Trusting, such as believing in others based on your own personal observations; Respecting, such as treating others as you would have them treat you; and Negotiating Differences such as being willing to compromise. These are all choices of behaviors you can use with others to make yourself happy. What others do to make themselves happy is their choice. This is happiness from a Choice Theory Perspective.

A final thought to close this book about happiness is in the timeless words of William Glasser, "I predict that everyone reading this booklet has had bad experiences with the deadly habits. If you even begin to replace them with a few of the caring habits, especially, respect, you will immediately feel a distinct improvement in the quality of your life."

Further Reading

Books by William Glasser, M.D.

All of Dr. Glasser's books can be viewed and are available from www.wglasserbooks.com or from booksellers everywhere and as e-books from Amazon

A Recommended Sample of Dr. Glasser's Best Selling Books:

Choice Theory: A New Psychology of Personal Freedom (also sold as an audio-book)

Take Charge of Your Life: How to Get What You Need With Choice Theory Psychology

Getting Together and Staying Together

Positive Addiction

For Parents and Teenagers: Dissolving the Barriers between Them

Counseling with Choice Theory, the New Reality Therapy

Warning: Psychiatry can be Hazardous to Your Mental Health

Recommended Books By Carleen Glasser

Published by William Glasser, Inc. and available from: www.wglasserbooks.com

My Quality World Workbook. revised edition (2017) and
Glasser Class Meetings: Choice Theory Curriculum

Also Recommended:

Roy, J. (2014). William Glasser : *Champion of Choice*. Phoenix, AZ: Zeig,Tucker & Theisen.
        The William Glasser, M.D. Biography

Wubbolding, R. (2017). *Reality Therapy and Self-Evaluation: The Key to Client Change*.
Alexandria,VA: American Counseling Association.

The Choice Theory in Action Series Titles

A Choice Theory Psychology Guide to Addictions: Ways to Overcome Substance Dependence and Other Compulsive Behaviors - Michael Rice

A Choice Theory Psychology Guide to Anger Management: How to Manage Rage in Your Life - Brian Lennon

A Choice Theory Psychology Guide to Depression: Lift Your Mood - Robert E. Wubbolding, Ph.D.

A Choice Theory Psychology Guide to Happiness: How to Make Yourself Happy - Carleen Glasser

A Choice Theory Psychology Guide to Parenting: The Art of Raising Great Children - Nancy S. Buck Ph.D.

A Choice Theory Psychology Guide to Relationships: How to Get Along Better with The Important People in Your Life - Kim Olver

A Choice Theory Psychology Guide to Stress: Ways of Managing Stress in Your Life - Brian Lennon

The Choice Theory in Action Series is available from Amazon as e-books or paperbacks and may be obtained through bookshops including www.wglasserbooks.com

William Glasser International

The body that Dr. Glasser approved to continue teaching and developing his ideas is William Glasser International.

This organization helps coordinate the work of many member organizations around the world.

WGI recently introduced a six-hour workshop entitled, "Taking Charge of Your Life". This is intended for the general public and provides a good foundation in Choice Theory psychology.

If you are interested in further training in Choice Theory psychology or any of its applications, you are recommended to contact WGI or your nearest member organization of WGI.

www.wglasserinternational.org

Made in the USA
Middletown, DE
26 May 2023